Friendship

The Joy of Relationships

Martin Murphy

Friendship

Published by:
Theocentric Publishing Group
1069A Main Street
Chipley, Florida 32428

www.theocentricpublishing.com

Library of Congress Control Number: 2015904983

ISBN 9780986405518

To
My Special Friend
Mary,
With Love

Preface

This condensed book was written so the reader will be able to grasp the principles without having to go back and re-read it to digest the content. Friendship is a popular concept. Having a large number of friends was popularized by the social media such as Twitter and Facebook. Contrary to the popular notion, friendship involves a relationship of distinction. It is a relationship that respects the dignity of another person. The Bible teaches a different version of what it means to be a friend than the popular culture teaches. There are many occasions when friends say they are friends, but they are not friends. "Even my own familiar friend in whom I trusted, who ate my bread, has lifted up his heel against me" (Psalm 41:9). A true friend will endure and sacrifice for a friend. "A friend loves at all times" (Proverbs 17:7) and "there is a friend who sticks closer than a brother" (Proverbs 18:24). This monograph is as much rational as it is affectionate. The truth of biblical friendship will engage the entire person, mind, will, and emotions.

Table of Contents

1. Friends in Real Life

Social media technology has captured the attention of the public by misrepresenting the term "friend" and the concept known as "friendship." Facebook is a good example of the misuse of the word "friend." On Facebook the term "friend" may simply refer to a name, not a person.

The word "friend" is often used in the Bible in a variety of circumstances. Rather than try to explain each Hebrew and Greek word translated into English as "friend" a brief summary will suffice. Friends are two or more people in a unique personal relationship. For instance, Jesus was "a friend of tax-gatherers and sinners" (Matthew 11:19), however there is no mention of Jesus being friends with the religious leaders of His culture. Friendship will always find joy in unique relationships.

True friends are scarce. The old cynic who went about in broad daylight with a lighted lantern in search of a friend would have difficulty finding a true friend. It has often been said, "I went out to find a friend, but could not find one. I went out to be a friend and friends were everywhere." How does the Bible relate the concept of friendship to real life? The Bible is as up to date as the newspaper.

A friend is like a whetstone that gives keenness to the edge of energy and life. The Bible uses the adage, "Iron sharpens iron, so one man sharpens another" (Proverbs 27:17). There are many examples of friendship in the Bible. David and Jonathan, Ruth and Naomi, or perhaps Paul and Timothy are examples, just to mention a few. A friend can encourage if life issues are difficult, wearisome, or painful. A friend can comfort and advise during the trials of life. Friends make up for each other's defects and they delight in their relationship.

Friends not only learn from each other, they help each other develop character. Friends demonstrate faithfulness to one another.

Friendship

Sacrifice is the essence of friendship. The story is told of a soldier who asked his officer if he might go out into the "no man's land" between the trenches in World War I to bring in one of his comrades who lay grievously wounded. "You can go" said the officer, "but it is not worth it. Your friend is probably dead and you will throw your own life away." But the man went. Somehow he managed to get to his friend, hoist him on to his shoulder, and bring him back to the trenches. The two of them tumbled in together and lay in the trench bottom. The officer looked very tenderly on the rescuer and then he said, "I told you it wouldn't be worth it. Your friend is dead and you are mortally wounded." The soldier replied "it was worth it." "How was it worth it" asked the officer? The soldier replied, "it was worth it because when I got to him he was still alive, and he said to me, 'Jim I knew you'd come.'" Encouragement and faithfulness demonstrate the value of a friend. Be a friend, it's worth the effort.

The fourth chapter of John is an account of Jesus as he encountered a woman at the well of Samaria. The Samaritans were despised by the Jews, but Jesus being a Jew, was favorable to them. As a matter of fact when Jesus went to Samaria, he went about to explain the gospel to a Samaritan woman. This woman was living in an adulterous relationship and, no doubt, a disgrace to the community. Little did it matter to Jesus that this woman was a social low-class. Did social peer pressure keep Jesus from going to Samaria? No! He went to Samaria to be a friend to the Samaritans.

This past century produced an abundance of literature about the subject of friendship. Much of it has been and still is under the heading of relational theology. This is an approach to Christianity that stresses the relationship of persons to persons rather than a direct relationship to God through Jesus Christ by the power of the Holy Spirit. A favorable relationship with God precedes friendship with one another.

Religious leaders have been very successful in propagating this psychological concept, but it proves to be counter-productive because it denigrates the doctrine of God and elevates the doctrine of man.

God created human beings to be rational social beings, therefore friendship is necessary on all levels of society. However, there is a common mistake in society. The biblical sense of friendship may be absorbed by a utilitarian arrangement or to say it another way, friendship is merely for convenience. People want to be friends and have friends because of the advantages afforded by the friendship itself. That is not biblical, nor is it a principle of ethics that is normative in any sense. Friendship results from the desire to serve, not to be served. However, biblical friendship may be interrupted by human emotions such as anger.

2. Friends Challenged by Anger

The word "anger" or "angry" is a condition of the mind and expression of human emotions. It is about as hard to define as the word "love." A brief summary of biblical instruction will show anger is not merely a communicative expression. Anger is not merely facial contortions or the volume of one's vocal expression or any composure that seems displeasing to the recipient. Some people equate anger with contemptuousness and contentiousness. Contemptuousness refers to an arrogant and defiant person. Contentiousness refers to hostility and strife. Anger is a biblical concept associated with that dimension of the soul known as the "affections" in previous centuries, but now generally referred to as the "emotions." Any expression of the emotions may be sinful or it may be righteous. The only way sinful men, and all men are sinful, may interpret an emotional concept is to understand the biblical teaching of that particular concept, whether it is love, anger, hate, et al.

Dr. Jay Adams, founder of the Nouthetic Counseling Movement, describes biblical anger. "The energies of anger are wasted and used damagingly when they are directed solely toward oneself or another. Under control, anger is to be released within oneself and toward others only in ways that motivate one to confront others in a biblical manner in order to solve problems. Anger is a powerful emotion. But its power to motivate must be used, not abused. This motivating power is used properly when it drives one to begin to rectify any wrong situation between brethren as quickly as possible. It is used biblically when it impels one to become reconciled to his brother immediately" [Matthew 5:22] (The Christian Counselors Manual, p. 354 and 355). So in the final analysis when someone is charged with sinful anger, it means the angry person intends to inflict pain, harm, and/or damage on a person, rather than deal with the problem that originally caused the anger. Friends should remember the sound biblical instruction: "Let all bitterness and wrath and anger and clamor and slander be put away from you, along with all malice" (Ephesians 4:31).

3. Friends Wounded by Slander and Gossip

Gossip is another wedge that separates friends. Gossip and slander is the cause of many broken friendships. Gossip is most often associated with someone spreading a rumor, which means a story, or statement is circulated without any confirmation or certainty. Slander is a false or defamatory statement.

The Bible always uses the word "gossip" in a bad sense. In 1 Timothy 3:11 women are told not to be malicious gossips. In 2 Timothy 3:3 the word "malicious gossip" is used universally to apply to men and women. The Greek word *diabolos* translates to the English "gossip" in both texts. The Greek word *diabolos* is also translated "the devil" thirty four times in the New Testament. The English word "diabolic" is derived from the Greek *diabolos*. The apostle Paul intended to convey the wickedness of "malicious gossip" in his letters to the churches.

The Bible uses the word "slander" in a negative sense. In fact the wisdom writer has said: "He who spreads slander is a fool." The Psalmist said: "The fool has said in his heart, no God." In either case the fool has no positive witness for the Lord God Almighty. Slander is particularly detestable because it has the smell of murder. To slander a person and destroy his name is not just a violation of the ninth commandment, but also the sixth commandment.

Gossip and slander are common sins. However, because of the nature of these sins, they are very difficult to control. If the gossip and slander is within the confines of the church, reconciliation is relatively simple. Just follow the instructions in Matthew 18.15-20.

However, if the gossip is spread from within the church to those out of the church, it is merely hearsay and the third party outside the church refuses to reveal the spreader of the gossip, so the church suffers because of the sin of one or more of its members.

Gossip and slander have an advocate and his name is Satan. He deceives people into thinking that it is permissible to gossip and slander and therefore breaking the sixth and ninth commandments. John Calvin mentions a more applicable purpose in his commentary to 1 Timothy 5:19: "He now tells Timothy not to let them [elders] be exposed to slanderous attacks or burdened with unsubstantiated and unsupported accusations... . For none are more to guard against malice of men in this way. For none are more exposed to slander and insults than godly teachers ... . It is indeed a trick of Satan to estrange men from their minister so as gradually to bring their teaching into contempt." The apostle Peter inferred that Christians would be slandered as evildoers (2 Peter 2:12). The Psalmist said no less in Psalm 41:5: "My enemies speak evil against me... ."

Godly ministers, elders, deacons, and church members will be the subject of gossip and slander if they preach, teach, and believe the full counsel of God. It may be properly called the "battle of the tongues." The godly man seeks the truth from the Word of God. The slanderous man wants to have his own way apart from the Word of God. Since truth is not on his side, he must lie to get a hearing. The writer of Proverbs explains: "A worthless man digs up evil, while his words are as a scorching fire. A perverse man spreads strife, and a slanderer separates intimate friends" (Proverbs 16:27-28).

Gossip and slander are terrible sins, but they are not unforgivable sins unless they are against the Holy Spirit. When the gossiper or slanderer becomes aware of his or her sin, he or she must immediately ask forgiveness from the person about whom he or she spread the gossip or slander. Anger, gossip and slander should not disturb the relationship between friends, if they follow the biblical doctrine of forgiveness.

4. Friends Forgive and Reconcile

Friends following biblical instructions on the doctrine of forgiveness will always have mutual favorable relations with one another. Friendship and forgiveness go hand in glove. A brief look at the doctrine of forgiveness reveals the primary agent for enjoying friendship.

Do you ever feel guilty? The word "guilt" means that some punishment is due for some unlawful action or behavior. People are born guilty, because they inherit the guilt of Adam's sin. Although God created Adam a perfect man, Adam sinned and the guilt of his sin passes on to all people. "Behold, I was brought forth in iniquity, and in sin did my mother conceive me" (Psalm 51:5). You not only inherited Adam's sin nature; you also practice sin against God and against other people. "Everyone who practices sin also practices lawlessness; and sin is lawlessness" (1 John 3:4). The Bible affirms, "all have sinned and fall short of the glory of God" (Romans 3:23). When people sin against God, there is a broken relationship. When people sin against each other, there is a broken relationship. The only way to have the guilt removed and restore the relationship is to pay for the sin or have someone else pay the penalty for you. Your sin erects a wall between you and God. Sin severs the relationship between God and man. The only remedy for that separation is forgiveness. Is there any forgiveness? Yes, through the shed blood of the Lord Jesus Christ who paid the penalty of death for God's children.

Sin causes guilt. Forgiveness is the only way to relieve the guilt and heal the broken relationship. It is the guilt of sin that burns in the human heart. So, how is the guilt removed? Confession, repentance and forgiveness are the instruments to remove it. Martin Luther said, "forgiveness of sins through Christ is the highest article of our faith." The reason Luther said that is because of his understanding of God's holiness and man's sinful heart. You may take great comfort in the inspired words of the apostle Paul. "God has reconciled us to Himself through Jesus Christ and given us the ministry of reconciliation" (2 Corinthians 5:18).

The only way to know how to forgive is to model our forgiveness after God's forgiveness. The biblical instruction is, "be kind to one another, tenderhearted, forgiving one another, even as God in Christ forgave you" (Ephesians 4:32).

God's pattern of forgiveness in the Bible begins with confession. "If we confess our sins, He is faithful and righteous to forgive us our sins and to cleanse us from all unrighteousness" (1 John 1:9). Confession is essential for forgiveness because confession is the means of verbalizing the offense. Repentance is also necessary for forgiveness. "Be on your guard! If your brother sins, rebuke him; and if he repents, forgive him" (Luke 17:3). Repentance is a change of mind and endeavor to turn to God in obedience. To put it another way, repentance is a change of attitude and direction.

Christians pattern their forgiveness after God by saying, "I will forgive their wickedness and remember their sins no more" (Jeremiah 31:43). God does not say He will forget their sins, thus denying the fundamental doctrine of omniscience, but He will not remember them. In other words He will not bring them up again. If someone says I can forgive but I can't forget, then that person is not following the pattern of God's forgiveness. "As far as the east is from the west, so far has he removed our transgressions from us" (Ps. 103:12). Feelings do not determine the reality of forgiveness. What counts is objective reality, which is found in the Word of God. We must judge with truth, not how we feel about truth. God does not forgive because He feels like it. God forgives because of His grace and mercy.

Does anyone deserve forgiveness? The biblical doctrine is, "If you O Lord, kept a record of sins,

O Lord who could stand?" (Psalm 130:3). God, by His pure grace, forgives you of your multiplied sins against Him. If you believe in the forgiveness of sins you believe that you have been forgiven of the thousands upon thousands of sins that have been removed by the sacrifice of the Lord Jesus Christ.

Therefore, you must pattern your forgiveness after God's forgiveness. To forgive the other person means to remove from your mind any wrath, hatred, or desire for revenge. To forgive means to willingly, gladly, generously, and finally forget any injustice you may have experienced in your relationships with other people. Forgiveness means that the sin will never be brought up again and the relationship is restored, thus reconciliation of the two parties. God promises to forgive, but woe to the person who refuses to forgive and be reconciled.

When we practice or refuse to practice the biblical doctrine of forgiveness, it is evidence of a spiritual condition. Mutual forgiveness is necessary for reconciliation. The doctrine is very clear. God, by His pure grace, forgives you of your multiplied sins against Him, then you must forgive others who sin against you. When you forgive, truly forgive, you are simply following the example of your Lord and give evidence of the grace of the Lord Jesus Christ present in your soul. If you are not able to forgive others who have offended you and sinned against you, then you have not received any forgiveness from God. The Lord says, "For if you forgive men their trespasses, your heavenly Father will also forgive you. But if you do not forgive men their trespasses, neither will your Father forgive your trespasses" (Matthew 6:14).

The result of forgiveness is reconciliation of two or more people who were previously disenfranchised from each other. Reconciliation is not optional. Reconciliation means peace. Do you want peace with God and peace with other Christians? If the answer is yes, I urge you to remember the words of the Psalmist. "I acknowledged my sin to Thee, and my iniquity I did not hide; I said, I will confess my transgressions to the Lord; And Thou didst forgive the guilt of my sin "(Psalm 32:5).

Christian friends should desire worship and fellowship with other Christian friends who believe in the biblical doctrine of forgiveness and reconciliation. The one word everyone should desire to be on their headstone is: Forgiven.

5. Friends Love Each Other

Friends love one another. The first time the word "love" is used in the Old Testament it describes Abraham's affectionate relationship with his only son Isaac (Genesis 22:2). The last use of the word "love" in the Old Testament is a mandate from the Lord to "love truth and peace" (Zechariah 8:19). Likewise in the New Testament love is associated with relationships, affections and truth. The meaning of love is not limited to human emotions, but rather love comes from the mind and the will of the soul. The extent of its meaning is sometimes best understood when compared to the opposite end of the spectrum; love stands in opposition to hate. Love and hate are basic attitudes of life. "Hatred stirs up dissension, but love covers over all wrongs" (Proverbs 10:12).

The apostle Paul describes love as the most excellent way (1 Corinthians 13). The most excellent way hopes all things, endures all things and never fails. Did Paul say "love never fails?" Paul describes love biblically, while the contemporary culture defines love in terms of affection, approval, attraction, and so on but they all fail at some point. When Paul says love never fails he must mean divine love. The love of God never fails. The love people have for one another fails to a greater or lesser degree at one time or another.

Jesus issued the commandment to love one another, which is related to the Old Testament commandment to "love your neighbor as yourself" (Leviticus 19:18). Jesus issued this commandment because love was a principle He lived and died for. The love of Christ is pure love and it is free of prejudice. He prayed for the ones who murdered him because His love for them was free of prejudice.

Jesus gave the commandment to love one another because it would show evidence of the new spiritual birth. "We know that we have passed from death to life because we love our brothers" (1 John 3:14). Spiritual regeneration is one of the theological implications of brotherly love. It is also evidence of spiritual growth.

Love one another is a reciprocal command. Friends must mutually love each other. The injunction to love one another ought to be the desire of the heart; Not under compulsion, but freely with a merciful heart. Love ought to over-flow for each other (1 Thessalonians 3:12).

If Christian friends meditate on the command to "love one another" it will always lead to the desire for the well-being of the other person. Rather than acting on self-interest, Christian friends who love one another will act in the sole interest of the other person.

Love is inseparably connected with other aspects of the Christian life. It has been said that love is the father of justice. Justice requires pure and true love which is found in the Lord Jesus Christ. If love is the father of justice, then love is the mother of truthfulness. Christians are not able to deceive those they truly love. The connection between truth and love is inseparable. Love comes before mercy and gives the faint hearted patience to finish the race. Love is the main spring that gives the believer courage and strength to follow God.

Christians must love God in response to His love for them, and they are to love each other as a result of their love for God. "We love, because He first loved us. If someone says, 'I love God,' and hates his brother, he is a liar; for the one who does not love his brother whom he has seen, cannot love God whom he has not seen. And this commandment we have from Him, that the one who loves God should love his brother also" (1 John 4:19–21, NASB).

Love is the energy of the soul expressed by human affections and action directed to the beloved. Jonathan Edwards made a statement about love that comforts the soul. "But when love is in lively exercise, persons don't need fear, and the prevailing of love in the heart, naturally tends to cast out fear" (Letters and Personal Writings of Jonathan Edwards, Yale edition vol. 16, p. 94).

6. Friends Encourage Each Other

Friends will encourage one another. Christians need to encourage one another for many reasons. Encouragement is needed because the Word of God says, "all who desire to live godly in Christ Jesus will suffer persecution" (2 Timothy 3:12). The promise from Scripture is that a godly compassionate relationship with other Christians will bring comfort and relief. When Christians experience various and sundry troubles in life (Job 5:7), the need to encourage one another is the balm of relief.

Christian friends need to encourage one another with sound doctrine. The apostle Paul charged Timothy to, "Hold fast the pattern of sound words which you have heard from me, in faith and love which are in Christ Jesus" (2 Timothy 1:13). This verse has three grammatical considerations when examined separately will help Christians understand the entire verse. The command is have or to hold fast. The pattern is a summary account or an outline. Sound words are healthy words, good for the health of the soul.

Paul literally instructed Timothy to have an outline of healthy words inspired by God the Holy Spirit. The only way Christians should teach one another is with sound doctrine and that requires using sound words. The sound words found in the Word of God are good for the soul. Therefore, healthy words from the Word of God will result in a healthy soul when Christians receive them in faith and love. Sharing the Word of God is the best way for friends to encourage one another.

7. Friends Pray for Each Other

The Book of James commands Christians to "pray for one another" (James 5:16). Prayer for Christian friends should come as natural as breathing. Although this is in the form of a commandment, the evidence from the corpus of Scripture is that Christians should pray for one another without being commanded by God. It just seems natural for friends to pray for one another. The essential meaning of the word "pray" and "prayer" is to call on God or go before God in confession, praise and petition. Prayer for one another should reflect the interest each one has for the sanctification of the other. There are too many occasions that some professing Christians turn to God with prayer only in the case of an emergency when all other efforts to protect life or property fail. Prayer is a mutual duty to each other. The "pray for one another" doctrine is found in the Lord's model prayer.

Jesus said the model for prayer is "our Father...give us...our daily bread...lead us...deliver us" (Luke 11:1-4). It is not me or mine, but rather a mutual concern that causes "us" to pray for one another. The commandment is "pray for one another," Christians ought to delight in praying for the members in the family of God. Friends should give special attention to pray for one another.

8. Friends Forever

Where does friendship end? There is no end to friendship. It only has a beginning. Older friends may depart and go to be with God, but the friendship remains. New friends must be made because there is always a desire for friendship to fulfill an emptiness often known as loneliness. True friendship has no end. The Bible refers to Abraham's friendship to God forever (2 Chronicles 20:7). The friends of God are friends forever.

Enrich your life by looking for friendships the way Jesus looked for them. He went to "out of the way" places like Samaria. He sought to be a friend to people regardless of their demeanor or circumstances in life. Using the biblical principles of friendship could change the witness of the church and change the culture with a new reformation. An English publication offered a prize for the best definition of a friend, and among the thousands of answers the winner defined a friend. "A friend, - the one who comes in when the whole world has gone out." Go to Samaria and be a friend.

About the Author

Martin Murphy has a B.A. in Bible from Columbia International University and Master of Divinity from Reformed Theological Seminary. Martin spent nearly thirty years in the class room, the pulpit, the lectern, the study, and the library. He now devotes most of his time consolidating academic and practical gains by writing books. He and his wife Mary live in Dothan, Alabama. He is the author of eleven Christian books.

The Church: First Thirty Years, by Martin Murphy, 344 pages, ISBN 9780985618179, $15.95. This book is an exposition of the Book of Acts. It will help Christians understand the purpose, mission, and ministry of the church.

The Dominant Culture: Living in the Promised Land, by Martin Murphy, 172 pages, ISBN

970991481118, $11.95. This book examines the culture of Israel during the period of the Judges. It explains how worldviews influence the church and it reveals biblical principles to help Christians learn how to live in the culture.

My Christian Apology, by Martin Murphy, 98 pages, ISBN 9780984570874, $7.95. This book investigates the doctrine of Christian apologetics. It explains rational Christian apologetics.

The Essence of Christian Doctrine, by Martin Murphy, 200 pages, ISBN 9780984570812, $12.95. This book was written so that pastors and layman would have a quick reference to major biblical doctrines. Dr. Steve Brown says it was written, "with clarity and power about the verities of the Christian faith and in a way that makes a difference in how we live."

Return to the Lord, by Martin Murphy, 130 pages, ISBN 9780984570805, $8.95. This book is an exposition Hosea. The prophet speaks a message of repentance and hope. Hosea's prophetic message to Old Testament and New Testament congregation is "you have broken God's covenant; return to the Lord. Dr. Richard Pratt said "We need more correct and practical instruction in the prophetic books, and you have given us just that."

Theological Terms in Layman Language, by Martin Murphy, 130 pages, ISBN 9780985618155, $8.95. This book is written so that simple words like faith or not so simple words like aseity are explained in plain language. Theological Terms in Layman Language is easy to read and designed for people who want a brief definition for theological terms. The terms are in layman friendly language.

Brief Study of the Ten Commandments, by Martin Murphy, 164 pages, 9780991481163, $10.95. This book will help Christians discover or

re-discover the meaning of the Ten Commandments.

The Present Truth, by Martin Murphy, 164
pages, ISBN 9780983244172, $8.95.   Each
chapter examines a topic relative to the Christian
life. Topics such as church, sin, anger, marriage,
education and more.

Doctrine of Sound Words: Summary of Christian Theology, by Martin Murphy, 423 pages,
ISBN 9780991481125, $16.95. One reviewer
said, "This is a truly readable and accessible
commentary with no peer."